Great Wedding Parties

By Donna Kooler

A LEISURE ARTS PUBLICATION

10   9   8   7   6   5   4   3   2   1

Library of Congress Cataloging-in-Publication Data
    Kooler, Donna
    Great Wedding Parties
    "A Leisure Arts Publication"

ISBN: 1-57486-209-X

Contributors

PRODUCED BY

KOOLER DESIGN STUDIO inc.

PUBLISHED BY

LEISURE ARTS

If you have questions or comments
please contact:

LEISURE ARTS CUSTOMER SERVICE
P.O. Box 55595
Little Rock, AR 72215-9633
www.leisurearts.com

KOOLER DESIGN STUDIO, INC.
399 Taylor Blvd. Suite 104
Pleasant Hill, CA 94523
kds@koolerdesign.com

COLOR SEPARATIONS AND DIGITAL PREPRESS
ADMAC Digital Imaging, Emeryville, CA

PRINTED IN THE U.S.A. BY
R.R. Donnelley & Sons, Co.

KOOLER DESIGN STUDIO

PRESIDENT: Donna Kooler
EXECUTIVE V.P.: Linda Gillum
VICE PRESIDENT: Priscilla Timm
EDITOR: Judy Swager
ILLUSTRATORS: Linda Gillum, Barbara Baatz
Sandy Orton, Tom Taneyhill
Nancy Rossi, Jorja Hernandez
STAFF: Sara Angle, Jennifer Drake
Virginia Hanley-Rivett
Marsha Hinkson, Arlis Johnson
Karen Million, Char Randolph

GREAT WEDDING PARTIES

CREATIVE DIRECTOR: Donna Kooler
BOOK DESIGN: Nancy Wong Spindler
WRITERS: Shelley Carda, Judy Swager
Sandy Orton, Linda Gillum
Joanne Lehrer
COPY EDITORS: Joan Cravens, Judy Swager
Kit Schlich
ILLUSTRATOR: Linda Gillum
PHOTOGRAPHERS: Dianne Woods, Berkeley, CA
Don Fraser, Berkeley, CA
PHOTO STYLISTS: Donna Kooler, Basha Hanner
Ina Rice
SUPPORT: Laurie Grant
Deborah Magers-Rankin
Joyce Gengler
Deanna Sheehan

Contents

Wedding Showers and Parties

WHEN AN ENGAGEMENT IS ANNOUNCED THE WORLD seems to burst into parties. The tradition of celebrating weddings is so old that even if we tried, we couldn't trace it back to the beginning. The start of a new family just begs for festivities.

Cavemen must have rushed out and bagged a mastodon to barbecue. Cavebrides probably fussed over the deplorable lack of choice in bridesmaids' pelts, while bridesmaids collected attractive rocks to surround the happy couple's new fire-pit and wove garlands for the groomsmen's clubs. And each of these activities would have been a party.

Have we changed much? Maybe not. In more recent times, parties have been held to celebrate virtually every step of the change from the single to the married state, down to coloring fingernails and cutting hair.

In bygone days ceremonies surrounding the bestowing of dowries and wedding gifts were solemn events because they determined the domestic comforts the bride would find in her new home as well as her social status. Often a girl spent much of her youth making what she needed for her own home. The fullness of her hope chest was the measure of her readiness for marriage.

America, with its rich blending of cultures, established new customs. In the untamed land there were few towns and often fewer relatives. With less wealth at hand, goods to equip a new household were gifts "showered" upon the bride-to-be at parties given by women who were not relatives, but who remembered what it was to be a new bride with little or nothing to set up housekeeping. These gifts of friendship were the beginning of the American tradition of bridal showers, given by loving friends to supply the little things so often overlooked in the rush to choose the china or silver.

Is a wedding greater than the sum of its parties? The question begs for experimentation, and fortunately there are ideas aplenty for the requisite research. We offer here our own guide to the engaging enterprise.

One of the delights of the pursuit of happiness is that there are no absolutes. Couples are as varied as the human population, and so are the festivities surrounding the happy nuptials. Parties are as personal as the beloved, as varied as the joys of married life, and as close at hand as the nearest crafts store. There is a celebration for every aspect of daily life, from the rising of the sun to the setting of the table, and any of these is a grand excuse for a party!

Consider the fun of collecting essential (or esoteric) kitchen implements for a kitchen shower. While you dally over lemon meringue tarts and fortify yourselves with classic chicken dishes, you can assemble for the engaged couple the absolute musts for creating their first breakfast together. Whisk away the bride-to-be on a cook's tour of gadgets and closely guarded recipes. After all, isn't the art of the perfect omelet one of the secrets of married life?

However, there is more to marriage than breakfast and an "Around the Clock" party is an idea whose time has come for people who are ready to celebrate every minute of the day or night. Dividing the day into timely gifts will provide hourly opportunities for happy memories, while a drop-dead chic menu will sustain the guests through the revels.

Why limit yourselves to the party palette of the past? While the formal engagement party is a delightful return to the quiet restraint of earlier times, with the gentle gleam of silver and the music of china plates, there are still party vistas to be explored and celebratory peaks to be scaled. Instead of one or two large parties, why not have several small ones, so that you can celebrate with many different people in intimate settings?

The garden is always an excellent source of inspiration for a shower. Ours is complete with clay pots to celebrate love in bloom and jars of pansies to mirror the smiling faces of the guests. Or maybe there is no time after the wedding for a lengthy honeymoon. Then relax and be restored by a sunny Mediterranean party before the wedding. Taste a zesty tapanade and, voilà! you are in sunny France for an afternoon.

"Many hands make work light," say the Dutch. You can prove that easily enough by providing delightful refreshments while asking your guests for the "favor of their company" while you borrow their hands one evening to make favors for the bridal festivities. Who could say no to aram sandwiches, pizza, and arts and crafts for entertainment?

In *Great Wedding Parties*, we offer you a wide choice of ideas and suggestions to inaugurate the beginning of the wedding festivities or to round them out. Whichever party you give, the essential ingredient is joy. Be lavish with that, and your celebration will become a happy memory for all for years to come. ৵

How to Plan a Party

Planning a party isn't really hard, but you have to pay attention to several things at once. Here are some tips to help you with the basics.

❧ **GUEST OF HONOR** Get a list of dates and times when the guest of honor will be available.

❧ **WHERE** Decide on the location. That determines the number of guests, possibly the date, and maybe even the food and activities.

❧ **WHO AND WHEN** If you plan to invite businesswomen, schedule the party during evening hours. For stay-at-home moms, schedule it when their husbands can take over babysitting, or hire babysitters to take care of the children. A weekend may be the only time available. An option may be to give two identical but separate showers, one on a weekday and one in the evening.

❧ **THEME** Choosing a theme will help you focus. Your theme will influence your menu, decorations, and activities.

❧ **NUMBER** Determine how many guests you can accommodate, not just for seating and dishes, but to serve comfortably by yourself. If you need help, ask your friends. Write out the guest list. Decide who will cook what.

❧ **SETTING THE SCHEDULE** Check with the guest of honor for available dates then decide absolutely the date, time, location, and helpers for the party. Tell your helpers to mark their calendars and change nothing after this point.

❧ **INVITATIONS** Send invitations four to six weeks before the event. Pretty invitations do not get mislaid. Include the date, time, location, theme, and the name of the guest (or guests) of honor. Ask for RSVPs, and allow two weeks for responses.

❧ **FOOD** Make a supply list and schedule the times when the various dishes must be prepared. This is essential if you are doing it all yourself so you don't overlook a dish. If your helpers are cooking, give them tested recipes.

❧ **DECORATIONS, FAVORS, AND GAMES** Make a list of supplies by group, such as refreshment table, gift table, ceiling, table favors, prizes, etc. and check them off when you have them. Store them together by group.

❧ **THE PARTY DAY** Put up hanging decorations a day before, if practical. Set the table first, then decorate the other areas. Hang the menu where you can mark off the dishes as they are served. Schedule time for a cup of tea an hour before the guests arrive. If you run late, teatime becomes useful time.

Engagement Party

TRADITION IS THE FOUNDATION OF CULTURE. NOWHERE is this more apparent than in the festivities marking human transitions. By tradition we reaffirm the continuity of life and hospitality, taking shelter from the demands of the modern world in time-honored ritual.

Wedding traditions are particularly strong because they mark transitions not just of individuals, but of entire families. Such customs connect us with our forebearers; formality honors our origins.

Far from being an annoyance, the etiquette of formal occasions allows us to slip easily into ritual behavior, helping us unite our modern selves with our ancestors. For a time, we put on behavior patterns of an earlier age, like antique clothing, and become richer and deeper than our individual histories. The solemnity of ritual occasions allows us to carry heritage gracefully. Upheld by etiquette, we become ambassadors of tradition.

The announcement of marriage plans is a perfect example of women reveling in formality. Since this intimate occasion frequently introduces unacquainted families to each other, guests are more at ease in a home setting. Women delight in the opportunity to dress up, set out the best china and

arrange the silver. They fill the crystal punch bowl and set out fresh flowers, candles, and an astonishing array of refreshments.

At the engagement party the parents' generation celebrates the next chapter of family history. Friends and relatives of the betrothed couple become acquainted, forming a new network of relationships as they share their children's histories of scraped knees, piano recitals, and practical jokes. The couple's only duties are to accept gifts and mingle, weaving two families into one.

Invitations to an engagement party can be as simple or formal as you wish, so long as they are elegant. Other showers and parties for the bride are lighthearted and casual; the engagement party is a foretaste of the wedding, requiring equal taste and refinement.

This party may be dressed as beautifully as a wedding,

at considerably less expense. Imagination is the key ingredient. The formal engagement party is a mother's dream for her daughter's wedding, in miniature. If the daughter is dreaming of a wedding straight out of the 21st Century, while mother has her heart set on a remake of "Gone With the Wind," the engagement party can be the happy compromise. If that clash of ideas doesn't exist, you can always use the occasion to experiment with a color scheme, a flower, or a tasty hors d'oeuvre. It will be even more memorable when it is echoed, perfected, at the wedding.

A wedding day is crowded with schedules and people and nerves. The well-planned engagement party anticipates all the happiness of a wedding, without the pressure. You can have your cake and eat it, too! ᧓

PARTY MENU

Champagne, white and red wine

Tea sandwiches★

Chocolate-covered strawberries★

Chocolate truffles★

Coconut macaroons★

Lemon bars★

Mini pumpkin cheesecakes

Assorted fruits

Coffee and tea

★*Recipe provided*

TEA SANDWICHES

(Makes 32 triangle sandwiches, serves 8)

1 loaf *pain de mie* or good-quality white bread

16 ounces cream cheese

½ cup heavy cream

¼ cup fresh tarragon or dill, chopped

1 bunch watercress

1 cucumber, peeled and thinly sliced

1 large or 2 small tomatoes, thinly sliced

Salt and pepper

With a fork or electric mixer, mix the cream cheese and heavy cream together until well blended. Mix in herbs and set aside. Wash and trim the watercress, discarding any tough stems and bruised leaves. Pair up two slices of bread for each sandwich. Spread two tablespoons herb cream cheese on each slice. Top one slice with watercress, cucumber or tomato as desired. Salt and pepper to taste. Cover with remaining slice. Trim crusts from sandwiches and discard. Cut each sandwich into four triangles and serve.

CHOCOLATE-DIPPED STRAWBERRIES

(Makes 30)

16 ounces dark, milk, or white chocolate

½ teaspoon corn syrup

2 quart-size baskets fresh strawberries (1½"-2" strawberries, approx. 2 pounds) with stems

2 cups assorted chopped nuts or mini-chips (optional)

4 ounces decorating chocolate, to contrast with dipping chocolate

Gently wash strawberries, discarding bruised or soft fruit. In the top of a double boiler, melt the chocolate and corn syrup together. Set aside for a few minutes to cool—it should not be hot.

Holding each strawberry by the stem; dip it into the chocolate. Let excess drain off, then wipe the tip of the strawberry against the pan. Roll some strawberries in nuts or mini-chips, if desired. Place on a parchment-paper-lined cookie sheet and chill.

To make decorative squiggles, warm the contrasting chocolate and pour into a clean, small squeeze bottle (a new hair coloring bottle is perfect for this). Squeeze zig-zag lines as desired. Store in a cool place until ready to serve.

CHOCOLATE TRUFFLES

(Makes 60 one-inch balls)

16 ounces semi-sweet or bittersweet chocolate, chopped

1 cup heavy cream

½ cup unsalted butter (1 stick)

1 tablespoon kirsch, framboise, or your favorite liqueur (optional)

1 cup cocoa powder

In a double boiler, combine the chocolate, cream and butter. Melt over low heat until all the ingredients are combined. Remove from the heat, and stir in the liqueur, if desired. Pour into an 8"-square pan and chill until cool.

Sift cocoa powder into a shallow bowl. Using a melon baller or teaspoon, scrape out a slightly rounded teaspoon of chocolate mixture; shape by gently rolling in the palm of your hand. Toss truffles in cocoa powder a few at a time; shake bowl gently until well-coated. Place on a waxed-paper-lined tray (single layer); chill. For ease in serving, place in candy cups or arrange on a plate. Truffles will keep in an airtight container in the refrigerator for two weeks.

LEMON BARS

(Makes approx. 24 two-inch squares)

For the crust

2 cups flour

⅓ cup powdered sugar

1 cup (2 sticks) butter, melted

For the filling

6 eggs

2½ cups sugar

1 cup lemon juice

½ cup flour

Powdered sugar (optional)

Grease or spray a 9" x 13" baking pan. Using a food processor, combine all the crust ingredients until they just hold together. Press into the pan and bake at 350 degrees until lightly browned, about 25 minutes. Meanwhile, make the filling.

Beat together the eggs and sugar until smooth. Stir in the lemon juice and flour. Pour onto baked crust and bake at 350 degrees until filling is just set, about 25 minutes. Cool and cut into squares. If desired, sift powdered sugar over the bars.

COCONUT MACAROONS

(Makes approx. 3 dozen)

4 egg whites, room temperature

⅔ cup sugar

¼ teaspoon salt

1 teaspoon vanilla

¼ cup flour

3 cups flaked sweetened coconut, lightly packed

3 ounces semi-sweet chocolate

½ teaspoon solid vegetable shortening

In large bowl, beat egg whites until foamy. Beat in sugar, salt, vanilla, and flour. Add coconut and stir until well combined.

Drop batter by rounded teaspoonfuls onto well-greased baking sheets, spacing cookies about 1" apart. Bake at 325 degrees for 20 to 25 minutes or until lightly browned. Let cool briefly on baking sheets, then transfer to racks and cool completely.

Melt the chocolate and shortening in the top of a double boiler over simmering water. Decorate cookies by either dipping one end in the chocolate or by drizzling chocolate from a spoon using a rapid back-and-forth motion to make thin chocolate stripes. Chill decorated cookies on a waxed-paper-lined tray until chocolate is set. Store in an airtight container.

Bridesmaids' Tea

THEY SMILE THROUGH THE SHOWERS. THEY KEEP THE flower girl from biting the ring bearer. And their dresses are often not their first choice. How much can bridesmaids stand?

To avoid finding out, give them a cup of tea. Give them the teapots, too. Even bridesmaids need to be catered to and fussed over now and then.

For their help in her rite of passage, the bride traditionally gives an intimate party for the bridesmaids, where she presents a gift to each in thanks for favors done and errands run and for the heroic duties of the wedding day. It's time for the ladies to rest and fortify themselves, and nothing fortifies, soothes, and cheers better than a tea party.

Start with simple, handmade invitations, as warm as a pot of tea. Use the art provided in this chapter, or design your own beautiful mementos. Decorate your party simply using lovely linens, pretty plates, and flowers like those painted on the teapots: roses, tulips, and poppies. Reflect glowing hearts with glowing candles.

The teapots are your chance to commemorate this time creatively. To each friend of your heart, her teapot says, "You are unique and irreplaceable. I treasure this time with you." The directions given here for making painted teapots are easy to follow. Be innovative, and express the feeling of the moment.

A simple tea is delightful. Delicious quiche and fresh fruit accompany scones bursting with currants. Mimosas stand ready for a celebratory toast to joy. The teapots will recall happy times together, no matter how far apart your futures take you. ༀ

BRIDESMAIDS' TEA INVITATION

CARD 1

SUPPLIES FOR EACH CARD:

(First, refer to Tips for Invitations on page 92.)

(Lavender) purchased envelope

(Yellow) heavy parchment paper

(Yellow checked) decorative paper

Color copy of teapot illustrations

⁵⁄₁₆"-wide (lavender) craft ribbon

INSTRUCTIONS

1. Cut a piece of heavy (yellow) parchment ¼" less than the width of the envelope but double the actual height.

2. Fold in one short side a little less than a third. Flip piece over to back. Cut out checked paper to fit back area.

3. Cut length of craft ribbon ½" longer than the height of the paper. Glue ribbon ¹⁄₁₆" in from short edge of (checked) paper; fold over ribbon ends to back of paper and glue down.

4. Glue (checked) paper to back of (yellow) parchment with the ribboned side aligned with the non-folded edge and all other edges matching.

5. Flip card unit over. Fold in ribboned side so that inside edge is ⅛" under larger flap, with most of ribbon width showing.

6. Cut out one large and one small teapot illustration. Glue large teapot on scrap of (yellow) parchment. Cut around, allowing an extra ¹⁄₁₆" border from edge of motif.

7. Glue large teapot on large flap of card; space as shown in photo. Glue small teapot to envelope flap.

BRIDESMAIDS' TEA INVITATION

CARD 2

SUPPLIES FOR EACH CARD:

(First, refer to Tips for Invitations on page 92.)

(Ecru) purchased envelope

(White) heavy card stock

(Light sand) paper

(White embossed) decorative paper

(Pink) card stock

Color copy of small teapot illustrations

⅜"-wide (pink) satin ribbon

Decorative-edge (lace) craft scissors

Double-stick foam mounting tape

INSTRUCTIONS

1. Cut a piece of (white) card stock ¼" narrower than the width of the envelope and double the height of the envelope minus ¼". Fold in half.

2. Using decorative-edged scissors cut a piece of (light sand) paper to fit within front of folded card, allowing about a ½" border. Center (light sand) paper on front of folded card and glue in place.

3. Cut a piece of (embossed) paper to fit within (light sand) paper, center and glue in place.

4. Cut a length of (pink) ribbon to fit within the (embossed) paper. Finish one end with a "V" cut. Center ribbon streamer on (embossed) paper as shown in photo and hot-glue top edge in place. Tie a (pink) ribbon bow and hot-glue to top of ribbon streamer. Trim each bow end with a decorative "V" cut.

5. Glue three small teapot illustrations to (white) card stock, then cut out, leaving ¹⁄₁₆" border from edge of motif.

6. Attach the teapots to ribbon streamer using small pieces of mounting tape and spacing them evenly as shown.

7. Cut out one teapot illustration with a ⅛" border. Glue to a piece of (pink) card stock, then cut out ⅛" beyond previous border. Glue to envelope flap.

PARTY MENU

Mimosas★

Spinach quiche★

Strawberries and crème fraiche

Cream scones★

Oatmeal scones

Lemon curd, clotted cream, Devonshire cream★

Angel food cake with strawberries

Assorted fruits

Coffee and teas

★Recipe provided

MIMOSAS

(Serves 8 six-ounce drinks)

1 bottle (750 ml) champagne or sparkling wine

1 quart fresh orange juice

1-2 limes, sliced paper-thin

Grenadine syrup (optional)

Fill a champagne flute halfway with fresh orange juice. Fill the rest of the glass with champagne. Add a splash of grenadine, if desired, for a beautiful pink color. Garnish with a slice of lime.

SPINACH QUICHE

(Makes one 10" quiche, serves 6-8)

For the crust

1¼ cups flour

½ teaspoon sugar

¼ teaspoon salt

½ cup butter (1 stick), cut into tablespoon-sized pieces

3-4 tablespoons ice water

For the filling

10-ounce package frozen chopped spinach, thawed

1 cup Gruyere or Swiss cheese, shredded

½ onion, finely chopped

1 tablespoon butter

3 eggs

1 cup cream

1 teaspoon fresh thyme leaves

¼ teaspoon salt

½ teaspoon pepper

For the crust, stir together the flour, sugar, and salt. Cut in butter using a pastry blender until dough clumps in pea-size pieces. (You can also use a food processor.) Add ice water all at once; mix until pastry starts to stick together. Roll out and press crust into the bottom and sides of a 10" tart pan with removable sides. Prick all over with a fork, and freeze for one hour. Preheat the oven to 375 degrees and bake the shell for about 25 minutes, until lightly browned.

For the filling, squeeze excess water from thawed spinach. Sauté the onion in butter until soft. Mix together the eggs, cream, and thyme, then add salt and pepper.

Scatter the spinach, then the onions, then the cheese on the bottom of the baked shell. Pour the egg mixture on top and bake for 30 minutes at 375 degrees. Serve warm or at room temperature. Garnish with a sprig of thyme.

CREAM SCONES

(Makes 16 scones)

4 cups flour

2 tablespoons baking powder

½ teaspoon salt

¼ cup sugar

½ cup butter (1 stick)

1 cup dried fruit—currants, raisins, chopped apricots or peaches, cherries, cranberries

2¾ cups heavy cream

Preheat the oven to 425 degrees. Line two baking sheets with parchment paper.

Sift together the flour, baking powder, and salt; add sugar. Cut butter into the flour using a pastry blender, or the lowest speed of your food processor, until well blended. (It will look like coarse breadcrumbs.)

Add the dried fruit and cream, and mix by hand just until the dough holds together (this is a very sticky dough).

Turn dough onto a well-floured board and cut in half. Pat each half into a circle about 9" in diameter. Cut each circle into eight pieces. Place the scones on a baking sheet and brush with cream. Bake approximately 20 minutes, until lightly browned.

Serve with jams, marmalades, quick clotted or Devonshire cream, or lemon curd.

QUICK CLOTTED CREAM

(Makes 2¼ cups)

1 cup heavy cream

2 tablespoons powdered sugar

½ teaspoon vanilla

½ cup sour cream, room temperature

Beat cream, sugar and vanilla with electric mixer until stiff peaks form. Gently fold in ½ cup sour cream, mixing until very thick. Chill until ready to serve.

QUICK DEVONSHIRE CREAM

(Makes 2 cups)

8 ounces cream cheese

1 teaspoon vanilla

3 tablespoons granulated sugar

¼ cup sour cream

¼ cup whipping cream

All ingredients should be at room temperature. Using an electric mixer, whip cream cheese until fluffy, then beat in remaining ingredients until well blended. Cover and refrigerate until serving time.

EASY OLD-FASHIONED LEMON CURD

(Makes 2 cups)

3 whole eggs

3 egg yolks

1 cup sugar

½ cup fresh lemon juice

¼ cup butter (½ stick) cut into pieces

½ teaspoon lemon zest

In a glass dish, combine the whole eggs, yolks, sugar, and lemon juice. Beat well then add butter. Place in the microwave and cook on high for three 1½ minute intervals, removing the dish and beating well after each 1½ minute interval. Add lemon zest. Curd should be silky smooth and thickened when done. Cover with plastic wrap and refrigerate.

Plain white teapots can be changed into rainbow-hued works of art to commemorate your bridesmaids' service on your wedding day. You may even want to make one for yourself. All you need are the simple instructions provided below. Feel free to allow your imagination to follow its fancy and your heart to write its own thoughts.

BRIDESMAIDS' GIFTS
Hand-painted Teapots
DESIGNED BY LINDA GILLUM

SURFACE: Blank teapot by *Pebeo,* 4¾" high x 4½" diameter (available in craft stores)

PALETTE: High Gloss Acrylic Enamel by *Liquitex Glossies*

Aqua	Pink
Black	Purple
Green	Red
Orange	White
Pine Green	Yellow Orange

BRUSHES:
½", ¾" flats
#6, #12 rounds
Small round

OTHER SUPPLIES:
Rubbing alcohol
Pencil
Ruler
Transfer paper (optional)

GENERAL INSTRUCTIONS:

Before painting, wash the teapot in hot soapy water; rinse in clean water and dry. Wipe the painting surface with rubbing alcohol to make sure it's totally grease-free.

Use a ¾" flat brush to paint all large areas. Allow each color area to dry before painting with a new color. To speed up the drying time, you may want to use a hair dryer. When all painting is complete, follow the manufacturer's instructions for drying and baking.

Refer to the color palette in the instructions for each teapot, then prepare the following color mixes as needed:

Sunny Yellow = Yellow + Yellow Orange + White

Medium Tangerine = Yellow Orange + Orange + White

Light Tangerine = Medium Tangerine Mix + White

Peach = Orange + White

Rose = White + Red

Light Pink = Pink + White

Medium Purple = Purple + White

Lavender = Medium Purple Mix + White

Light Aqua = Aqua + White

Dark Green = Pine Green + touch of White

Medium Green = Green + White + Pine Green

Light Green = Green + White

GREEN POLKA

PALETTE: Black, Lavender Mix, Light Green Mix, Peach Mix, Sunny Yellow Mix, White

1. Paint the body Light Green, the spout Sunny Yellow and the handle Lavender.
2. For the check pattern on the lid, first draw a pencil line around the lid about ¼" from the outside edge. Divide this area into equal sections making each check about ¼" wide and ¼" apart; be sure to keep a continuous pattern. Paint the checks Black, leaving the spaces between them unpainted. Paint a thin Black line along the top edge of the check pattern, following your pencil line.
3. Paint the rest of the lid (except knob) with Sunny Yellow, approaching the Black line carefully.
4. Complete the lid by painting the knob Peach.
5. Return to the main pot and use your pencil to mark the polka-dot pattern as shown. Paint dots White using the medium round brush.

FLORAL WHIRL

PALETTE: Black, Lavender Mix, Light Aqua Mix, Light Pink Mix, Medium Green Mix, Peach Mix, Sunny Yellow Mix

1. Paint the body of the teapot Sunny Yellow; let dry.
2. Paint the spout Peach and the handle Light Pink. Paint the top of the lid Light Aqua and the knob Light Pink.
3. Using a medium round brush, paint seven Medium Green leaves around the knob, starting at the base of the knob and extending almost to the top. Use a small round brush and Lavender to paint the ring around the neck of the knob.
4. Using a medium round brush and Black, scatter dots on the top of the lid as shown.
5. To paint the flowers at the base of the teapot, first use a pencil to mark the flower centers by evenly spacing four dots between the handle and the spout (repeat on other side). Leaving an area for the center of each flower, use a medium round brush and Lavender to make four short strokes forming the flower petals. For the leaves, use Medium Green to paint two slightly longer strokes on each side of the flower (see photo). Paint a large Peach dot in the center of each flower.

SOUTHWEST FIESTA

PALETTE: Black, Lavender Mix, Light Aqua Mix, Light Green Mix, Peach Mix, Sunny Yellow Mix

1. On the body of the pot, measure up about two thirds from the base, then use a pencil to draw a wavy line. Start at the handle, continue around above the spout, then back to the handle on the other side of the pot.

2. Paint the lower body of the pot Light Aqua. Paint the upper body Sunny Yellow. Using Peach and a medium round brush, loosely paint a thick and thin line where the two colors meet (follow your pencil line).

3. Paint the spout Light Green and the handle Peach. Using a medium flat brush, stroke across the outside edge of the handle with Sunny Yellow to create stripes.

4. Paint the lid Lavender and the knob Light Aqua. Use a narrow brush to paint a ring of Black at the base of the knob.

5. Return to the body and use a medium round brush to place a Black polka-dot pattern on the Sunny Yellow area as shown.

6. Using a pencil, draw a line ½" from the bottom of the teapot. Divide the area above and below the line into sections to form a checkerboard pattern. Sections above the line should be about ½" wide; sections below the line should be about ⅜" wide. Paint alternate squares with Black.

POPPY PARADE

PALETTE: Black, Lavender Mix, Light Green Mix, Light Pink Mix, Medium Green Mix, Medium Tangerine Mix, Peach Mix, Sunny Yellow Mix

1. Use a pencil to draw simple flower shapes in a random pattern on the body of the pot (see examples opposite). Or, trace the flower patterns and use transfer paper to apply them to the pot. Leave a comfortable space between the flowers, and also allow enough space for the leaves.

2. Choose one of the following colors for each flower: Peach, Light Pink, Sunny Yellow, or Lavender. Loosely paint the shape, allowing it to vary.

3. Place a large center in each flower using either Sunny Yellow or Medium Tangerine.

4. Add the leaf areas using a large round brush and Medium Green, loosely varying the size, shape and direction as shown.

5. With the medium round brush and Black, paint around the shapes, refining them as desired.

6. Paint the handle and spout Light Green, the lid Lavender, and the knob Sunny Yellow.

7. Use the medium round brush and Medium Green to paint the neck of the knob, then paint six leaves around the center of the lid, extending out from the neck of the knob as shown.

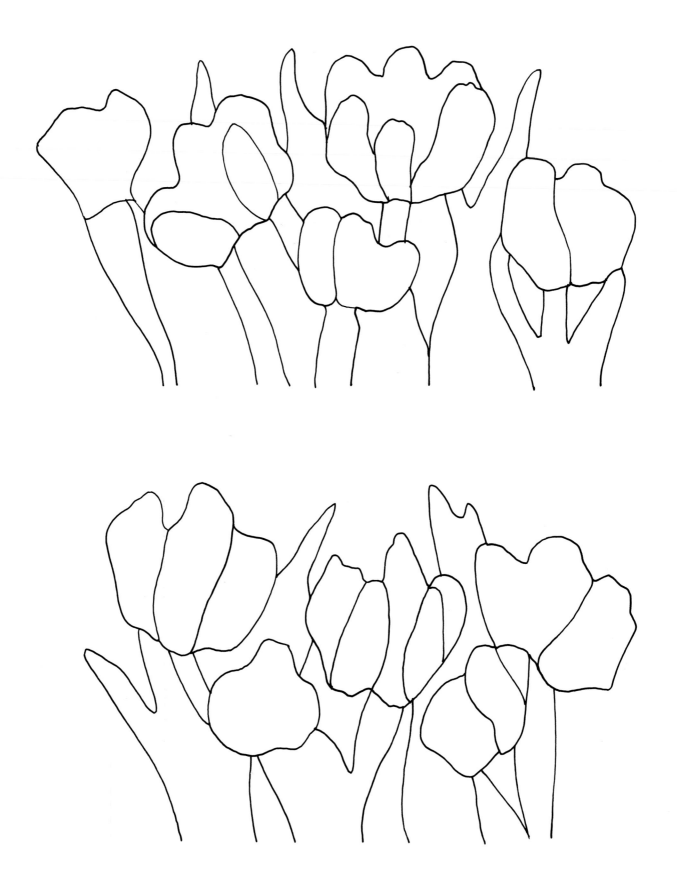

TANGERINE TULIPS AT MIDNIGHT

PALETTE: Black, Dark Green Mix, Lavender Mix, Light Green Mix, Medium Green Mix, Medium Purple Mix, Medium Tangerine Mix, Light Tangerine Mix,

1. This pot may be more challenging than the others, so you may prefer to transfer the pattern rather than paint freehand. Trace the pattern from the book; enlarge or reduce it as needed to fit your pot, and transfer with transfer paper.

2. Paint tulips Light Tangerine; add strokes of Medium Tangerine to most, but not all, flowers. Stroke from the base upward to create simple petal shapes.

3. Fill in the leaf areas using Medium Green. Create a second layer of leaves, stroking upward using Light Green, then add a few upward strokes of Dark Green.

4. Fill around the shapes using Black, correcting or improving them as desired.

5. Using a medium round brush, dab spots of Lavender and Medium Purple to create small accent flowers.

6. Paint the spout and handle Lavender.

7. Paint the lid Light Tangerine. Paint a swirling design on the lid using a medium round brush and Medium Tangerine. Start just below the neck of the lid and end at an outside edge.

8. Paint a polka-dot pattern on the knob using Light Tangerine.

ROSES IN THE SUN

PALETTE: Black, Dark Green Mix, Light Pink Mix, Rose Mix, Sunny Yellow Mix, White

1. Use a pencil to draw large rose shapes (see examples opposite) randomly on the body of the pot, referring to the photo for placement. Or, trace flower shapes from the pattern (opposite) and use transfer paper to transfer onto the pot.

2. Paint the flowers using Rose and the medium round brush. Add a small amount of White to the rose color; then, using the large flat brush, stroke at random over the top of each rose to loosely add dimension and variety. Loosely scribble petal lines in each flower using the medium round brush and Light Pink, allowing each flower to be different.

3. Draw simple leaf shapes between the flowers and paint them Dark Green.

4. Fill the unpainted areas using Sunny Yellow.

5. Paint the handle, spout, and lid Black. Paint the knob Rose; paint the pointed petal shapes from the neck up, using Light Pink and a small round brush. Paint a Dark Green ring around the neck of the knob.

6. Using the medium round brush, add Sunny Yellow polka-dots to the lid, spout, and handle as shown.

Kitchen Shower

EVERY BRIDE MUST KNOW ENOUGH ABOUT WHAT GOES ON in a kitchen to keep young love from starving or until she finds her husband enjoys culinary challenges more than she does. This is the purpose of a kitchen shower. It's fun, of course. Whisking out mysterious implements and guessing what they are used for is often hilarious. But what can be gleaned from a kitchen shower is considerably more than napkins, knives, and laughs.

The kitchen shower is a great time to coax beauty from the ordinary. What is more ordinary than fruit in a kitchen? But take a bowl of lemons, add a few daisies, place them in a sunny spot and they become an irresistible golden centerpiece. Or take a handful of humble wooden spoons, add a pretty ribbon, and you have a memorable gift. Suddenly the ordinary is significant.

Ladle beautifully colored fruit juices from a punch bowl and you please many senses at once. Toasted peaks of meringue on a lemon tart make a dessert too beautiful to eat… almost. Even simple cookie cutters filled with chocolate mirror hearts full of love.

Making something special out of the ordinary is the essence of marriage. It begins with basic equipment, without frills. We create the frills throughout our lives, and not just in the kitchen. So while you feast on lemon tarts and laugh about the tools of daily existence, remember that the ability to draw beauty from the ordinary is the key to contentment in all things. ৩

KITCHEN SHOWER INVITATION

SUPPLIES FOR EACH CARD:

(First, refer to Tips for Invitations on page 92.)

(Yellow) purchased envelope

(Blue and white plaid) paper

(Blue polka-dot) paper

(White) card stock

Color copy of knife, fork, and spoon illustration

¼" wide (yellow) silk ribbon

Double-stick foam mounting tape

INSTRUCTIONS

1. Glue illustration to (white) card stock, then cut out leaving a ¹⁄₁₆" border beyond edge of motif.

2. Cut a piece of (blue plaid) paper ¼" narrower than the width of the envelope and double the height of the envelope minus ¼". Fold in half. On the front of the card cut a square window a little larger than the height of the cut-out illustration (see photo).

3. Using the folded card as a pattern, cut a piece of (polka dot) paper. Glue paper, dot side showing through window, to the inside of (plaid) card, all outside edges aligned.

4. Attach illustration, using small pieces of mounting tape, centered within card front window as shown in photo.

5. Tie a (yellow) ribbon bow, sized as shown. Hot-glue in place where knife, spoon, and fork cross. Trim bow ends diagonally and glue in place as shown in photo.

PARTY MENU

Lemonade★
Assorted breads with herb butters
Caesar salad
Easy Chicken Divan★
Fruit plate
Lemon meringue tarts★

★Recipe provided

LEMONADE

(Makes approx. 8 16-ounce servings)
8 medium-sized lemons
1¼ cups superfine sugar
1 gallon water
Sour cherry, blackcurrant, or orange syrup
(optional)

Put the sugar into the pitcher or container. Juice 6 of the lemons and pour into the pitcher. Add 2 cups water and stir until the sugar is dissolved, then add remaining water. Slice the remaining two lemons and float them atop the lemonade. (If serving in a pitcher, slice just one lemon). You can also flavor the lemonade with fruit syrups (available at specialty foods stores and some grocery stores). For this, add sour cherry, black currant, or orange syrup, one tablespoon at a time, to taste.

EASY CHICKEN DIVAN

(Serves 8)

10-ounce can cream of chicken soup

10-ounce can cream of mushroom soup

12 ounces evaporated milk

1½ teaspoons curry powder

¼ cup lemon juice

2 pounds broccoli, cut into lengthwise strips and
steamed for 5 minutes

4 full chicken breasts, cooked and cut into
lengthwise strips

1½ cups raw mushrooms, sliced

3 cups jack cheese, shredded

½ cup bread crumbs and approx. a dozen
large purchased croutons

Mix together soups, evaporated milk, curry powder, and lemon juice until creamy. Butter a two-quart casserole dish, then layer half the broccoli, chicken, mushrooms and cheese. Pour half of the sauce over the layers. Add a second layer of broccoli, chicken, mushrooms, and cheese. Pour remaining sauce over top. Cover the top with bread crumbs and place large croutons around the edges. Bake in 350-degree oven until bubbly. Cool and refrigerate. Best when made ahead so flavors have time to blend. Reheat at 325 degrees for 45 minutes. Serve hot.

LEMON MERINGUE TARTS

(Makes twelve 4" tarts)

For the crust

    2 cups flour

    ¼ cup sugar

    ¾ cup (1½ sticks) butter, cut into pieces

    1 large egg, blended

Stir together flour and sugar. Using your fingers, pastry blender or an electric mixer, work butter into flour mixture until well-blended. Using a fork, stir in egg until dough holds together. Or blend flour, sugar, and butter in a food processor until mixture resembles fine crumbs: add egg and blend just until dough holds together.

Press dough into a ball. Wrap in plastic wrap and refrigerate for at least one hour or up to three days. Let come to room temperature before using.

Divide dough into 12 evenly-sized balls. Press dough into each tart pan, pushing firmly into bottom and sides to make an even layer. Use knife to cut edge of dough flush with pan. Place on baking sheet for ease in moving.

Preheat oven to 300 degrees. Bake tarts 20 to 25 minutes or until lightly browned. Let cool in pan. Invert pans and tap lightly to free shells, then turn cup side up. Store in an airtight container at room temperature for up to 4 days; freeze for longer storage.

For the lemon filling

    1½ cups sugar

    6 tablespoons cornstarch

    ¼ teaspoon salt

    ½ cup fresh lemon juice + ½ cup cold water
       (If using sweet Meyer lemons use 1 cup juice)

    3 well-beaten large egg yolks (reserve whites for topping)

    2 tablespoons butter

    1½ cups boiling water

    1½ teaspoons grated lemon peel

Sift sugar, cornstarch and salt into a medium saucepan. Gradually blend in water and lemon juice mixture, or all lemon juice. When smooth, whisk in the egg yolks and butter, blending thoroughly. Whisking constantly, gradually add 1½ cups boiling water.

Set pan over medium–high heat and stir until mixture boils, about 7 minutes. Reduce heat to medium and stir one more minute. Remove from heat and stir in grated lemon peel. Cover until ready to pour into shells after you have prepared the meringue topping.

For the meringue topping

¾ cup sugar

3 teaspoons cornstarch

6 large egg whites, room temperature

¼ + ⅛ teaspoon cream of tartar

In a small bowl, mix sugar and cornstarch; set aside. In a deep bowl, beat egg whites and cream of tartar using a mixer on high speed until very foamy and no liquid whites remain in bottom of bowl. Continue to beat at high speed, gradually adding the sugar-cornstarch mixture, one tablespoon at a time. Beat until whites hold stiff, glossy peaks.

To assemble tarts

Place tart shells on baking sheet for ease in moving. Fill with hot lemon filling. Spoon meringue onto filling. (When the filling is kept hot, the meringue is less likely to separate from it.) With a thin spatula, swirl meringue to cover filling and edge of crust completely. Use end of thin spatula to make decorative peaks.

Bake at 325 degrees until meringue is browned, about 15 minutes. Set tarts on rack until cool. Serve when cool or chill up to one day.

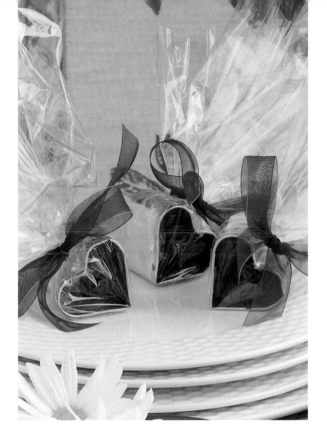

CHOCOLATE HEART FAVORS

SUPPLIES FOR EACH HEART:

Heart-shaped cookie cutter, 1½" x 1"

14" x 14" square clear cellophane

½"-wide organza ribbon, 16" length

Cookie sheets

Wilton's Candy Melts, light chocolate (12 ounce package fills 12 hearts)

Pastry or plastic bag

Small rubber bands

INSTRUCTIONS

1. Place cookie cutters on cookie sheet.

2. Melt chocolate following package directions. Pour into a pastry bag or heavy-duty plastic bag with small triangle cut from a bottom corner. Fill cookie cutters until chocolate reaches ⅛" from the top.

4. Place cookie sheet with cutters in refrigerator for several hours or overnight until chocolate has hardened.

5. Place filled cookie cutter point-side-down on center of cellophane square and gather up snugly to top. Secure with small rubber band.

6. Tie a bow using organza ribbon and snip ends to even up.

Around the Clock

CINDERELLA WAS NOT THE ONLY PERSON WITH HER EYE on the clock. From the first party to the last toast of the rehearsal dinner, an engaged couple races to get everything accomplished before the opening note of the Wedding March. At some point time must be made to stand still, and the bridal circle allowed some leisure.

The scene is set for this party, as dramatic as any palace ball. Invitations have been issued, with specially designed artistic flourishes. Champagne bottles are on ice. Tall flutes stand at attention. Elegant bites of caviar, smoked salmon, and crème fraiche whisper of the czar's palace. A black and white cake is the ultimate in sophistication.

Black and white define night and day. Clocks large and small abound, and reminders of the theme are everywhere, down to hourglass favors for the guests. Everything is poised for the revels to begin.

But the crisp and witty décor of this party belies the true nature of the evening. This is a party where any gift is appropriate, as long as you can link it to one of the hours of the day. Assign to each couple a specific time of the day or night, for which they are to choose a timely present: a hot water bottle for two o'clock in the morning, vintage martini glasses for the cocktail hour, an egg-poacher for daybreak.

Amidst such merriment and conviviality, time ceases to intimidate. What better, or more elegant, way to celebrate endless love? ॐ

AROUND THE CLOCK INVITATION

CARD 1

SUPPLIES FOR EACH CARD:

(First, refer to Tips for Invitations on page 92.)

(Flecked white) purchased envelope

(White) card stock

(Black and white checked) paper

Color copies of square arched clock face and
 sun/moon/clock group illustrations

¼" diameter silver cabochon (found in the jewelry
 findings and bead aisle of your craft store)

Fine-point, permanent black ink pen

INSTRUCTIONS

1. Cut a piece of (white) card stock ¼" narrower than the width of the envelope and double the height of the envelope minus ¼". Fold in half.

2. Cut a single row border from (checked border) paper to fit along three sides of the front of the folded card, and glue in place (see photo). Draw a borderline, using the fine-point black pen, ¹⁄₁₆" inside the checked border.

3. Glue illustration to a second piece of (white) card stock, then cut out ¹⁄₁₆" beyond edge of motif.

4. Glue cut illustration to front of folded (white) card, centered and spaced as shown in photo.

5. Glue cabochon to center of clock face.

6. Cut out sun/moon/clock group illustration ¹⁄₁₆" beyond edge of motif and glue to envelope flap.

AROUND THE CLOCK INVITATION

CARD 2

SUPPLIES FOR EACH CARD:

(First, refer to Tips for Invitations on page 92.)

(Metallic silver) purchased envelope

(Flecked white) card stock

(Black textured) medium weight paper

(Black and white checked) paper

Color copies of round clock face and sun/clock
   illustrations

⅜"-wide (black and white polka-dot) ribbon

Four ³⁄₁₆"-diameter silver cabochons (found in the jewelry
   findings and bead aisle of your craft store)

Double-stick foam mounting tape

INSTRUCTIONS

1. Cut a piece of (flecked white) card stock ¼" narrower
than the width of the envelope and double the height of
the envelope minus ¼". Fold in half.

2. Glue round clock face illustration to (flecked white)
card stock, then cut out ¹⁄₁₆" beyond edge of motif.

3. Cut a circle from (textured black) paper 1" larger than
cut clock face. Center (black) circle on front of folded
card and glue in place as shown in photo.

4. Glue clock face to center of (black) circle.

5. Attach four cabochons to the (black) circle, at posi-
tions shown in photo, using tacky craft glue.

6. Tie a (polka-dot) ribbon bow, sized as shown in photo.
Hot-glue bow, centering above (black) circle. Trim bow
ends diagonally and glue in place.

7. Cut out sun/clock illustration ¹⁄₁₆" beyond edge of
motif. Cut a square of (black checked) paper larger than
sun/clock. Glue sun/clock to center of (checked) square.
Glue unit to envelope flap.

PARTY MENU

Cocktails and champagne
Quick blini with smoked salmon,
caviar and crème fraîche★
Endive stuffed with gorgonzola and
topped with toasted walnuts
Smoked turkey on black bread
Curried deviled eggs
Ultimate chocolate cake★
Espresso, cappuccino, mocha

★Recipe provided

MORE EASY APPETIZERS:

❧ Prosciutto-wrapped figs

❧ Hummus with roasted red pepper spread on Belgian endive

❧ Mini-BLTs (Chop crisp bacon, tomato, lettuce, and avocado and add homemade or deli mayonnaise. Spread on bread. Cut off the crusts and cut into quarters. Cut each quarter in half on the diagonal.)

❧ Vegetarian sushi with wasabi dipping sauce

QUICK BLINI

(Makes about 18)

¼ cup (½ stick) butter

1¼ cups milk

1 cup all-purpose flour

¼ cup buckwheat flour (available at health food stores)

2 eggs

4 teaspoons baking powder

½ teaspoon salt

Warm the butter and milk together until the butter is melted. Set aside to cool. Sift together the flours, baking powder, and salt and set aside. When the milk mixture has cooled to room temperature, add the eggs and whisk together (this can also be done in a blender), then add the milk-egg mixture to the flours and stir until just combined. Preheat a griddle and grease lightly. Using a tablespoon, make 2"-diameter pancakes. Cook until bubbles appear on the top, and the pancake is nicely browned. Turn and cook for another minute. Keep warm in 300 degree oven.

Note: Although traditionally made with a yeast batter, these blini are much faster and just as delicious. They can be made ahead of time and rewarmed in a 350 degree oven at the last minute. Assemble quickly, so the blini will be warm when served.

For blini toppings

Crème fraîche or sour cream

2 ounces caviar (good quality, red or black)

8 ounces sliced smoked salmon, cut into slivers

1 bunch chives, snipped into small pieces

To assemble the blini

Top each blini with a teaspoon of crème fraîche or sour cream, about ½ teaspoon caviar, and a sliver of smoked salmon. Sprinkle with chives and serve.

increase speed to high, and beat for two minutes. Pour batter into pans and bake for 25-30 minutes, or until a tester comes out clean. Cool in the pan for ten minutes, then turn out and cool completely.

For white frosting

    1 cup milk

    5 tablespoons flour

    ½ cup butter

    ½ cup shortening

    1 cup granulated sugar

    1 teaspoon vanilla extract

Whisk together the flour and milk. Heat over medium heat until thickened, stirring briskly. Cool, then refrigerate until cold. Beat together the butter and shortening until light and fluffy. Add the sugar and vanilla. Gradually add the milk/flour mixture and beat until thick. Thin with a few drops of milk if needed.

For filling and glaze

    12 ounces semi-sweet or bittersweet chocolate

    1 cup cream

In the top of a double boiler combine cream and chocolate and melt together. Remove from heat. Set aside two thirds of the glaze to cool. Keep the remaining one third over the warm water for pouring over the cake.

To assemble cake

In the bowl of an electric mixer, whip the cooled chocolate glaze at medium speed until it lightens, (about one minute). Spread half of this filling over the bottom cake layer, saving the rest for decoration. Top with the second layer. Frost sides with white frosting. Carefully pour the warm glaze over the top of the cake, being careful not to let any drip down the sides; gaps at the edges can be hidden when decorating. Using a pastry bag with a decorative tip, pipe remaining whipped glaze around the base and top of the cake.

ULTIMATE CHOCOLATE CAKE

(Serves 8-12)

2 cups flour

2 cups sugar

¾ cups unsweetened cocoa powder

2 teaspoons baking soda

1 teaspoon baking powder

½ teaspoon salt

1 cup vegetable oil

1 cup milk

1 cup hot coffee

2 eggs

1 teaspoon vanilla

Preheat oven to 325 degrees. Butter and flour two 9" cake pans. Stir the dry ingredients together in the bowl of an electric mixer. Add the oil, milk, and coffee and beat at medium speed until combined. Add the eggs and vanilla,

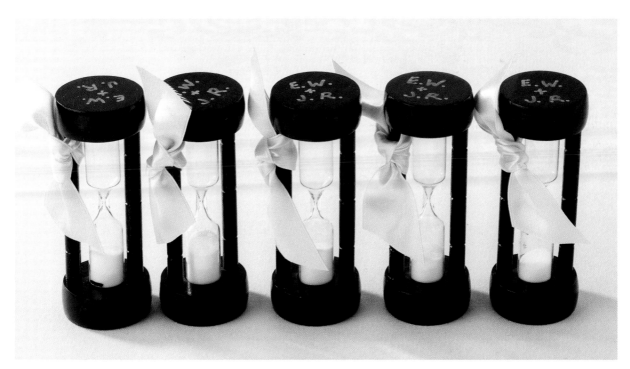

In just a flash you can transform an inexpensive egg timer into a clever favor—a timely gift for your guests to remember the evening's events.

TIMER FAVORS

SUPPLIES FOR EACH FAVOR:

3½"-high egg timers in wooden holder (available
    in craft stores in packages of 6)

Black glossy acrylic paint

Small round brush

5¼" of 1"-wide ivory satin ribbon

18kt.-gold-leafing pen

Scissors

INSTRUCTIONS

1. Paint the wood holder with black acrylic paint, carefully avoiding the plastic area. Allow to dry. Turn egg timer over and paint wood bottom. Allow to dry.

2. Personalize the top of the timer with the initials of the bridal couple using the gold-leafing pen.

3. Tie a double knot with the ribbon around one support bar of the timer. Clip ends of ribbon at an angle.

Deanna & Matt
September 11, 1999

Many Hands, Many Favors

"IS THERE ANYTHING I CAN HELP YOU WITH? ANYTHING at all?" You are sure to hear these words when you plan your wedding. Everyone loves the excitement surrounding a wedding, and people are caught up in the activity, or wish they could be. Turn this desire to join the fun into a social event.

You can do your relatives and friends an enormous favor while they are favoring you with their help—the favor of making favors! One brilliant gesture of practical hospitality will entertain a multitude while harnessing their enthusiastic energy.

With nothing but food and the materials for making your wedding favors, you can spend a delightful afternoon or evening, chatting and reminiscing while creating happy memories. At the same time, you can turn what might have been a lengthy chore into a festivity of the first magnitude. Just by wrapping almonds and creating commemorative bouquets you can entertain both adults and children.

The menu is simplicity itself. Beautiful aram sandwiches can be made in advance and whipped out when everyone is lagging. Pizza is popular with all ages, or treat your guests to that delicious new casserole recipe you plan to serve after the honeymoon. The fun and the favors will be finished all too quickly.

Years from now when the wedding bouquets are dusty and faded, the memories of your favor-making party will still be fresh. ॐ

SUPPLIES

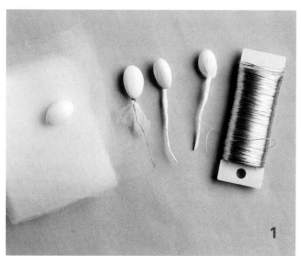

1

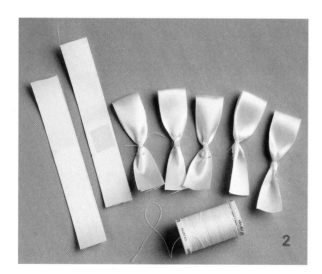

2

FAMILY FAVORS

Wedding favors serve as mementos of a couple's special day and are great for dressing up reception tables. This small gift from the bride and groom can be as simple or elaborate as you please: a decorated candle, a delicious chocolate in a personalized box, or a sachet-filled basket.

The traditional nosegay favor shown here was designed by Joyce and Deanna Gengler for Deanna's wedding to Matthew Sheehan. Drawing upon customs from her Italian heritage, Deanna's favors (also called "confetti") represent a wish for the newlyweds for prosperity and fertility; they contain three sugared almonds for good luck. From the time she was a little girl, Deanna remembered helping her Italian mother and grandmother make confetti for all the weddings and special anniversaries in the family.

Materials for her nosegay favors were purchased at a floral supply store and a party was planned for friends and relatives. At evening's end all admired the basket overflowing with favors awaiting the wedding day.

ALMOND NOSEGAY FAVORS

SUPPLIES FOR EACH FAVOR:
3 (lavender) ribbon mini-roses on stems
3 pearl stamen clusters
White mini-rose bouquet (wrapped bunch consisting of
   8 white ribbon flowers and 6 white satin leaves)
Lightweight floral wire
Three 4" squares of white tulle fabric
42" of 1"-wide white satin ribbon
28" of ⅜"-wide white satin ribbon
White thread
White florist's tape
3 sugared almonds
Hot glue gun
Printed message tag, 2¼" x ¾" on white card stock
Paper punch

INSTRUCTIONS

1. Center each almond on a 4" square of white tulle. Wrap the tulle around the almond, gathering it together at the pointed end of the almond; twist tightly. Wrap with lightweight floral wire to hold it in place, leaving about a 2" wire stem. Trim excess tulle, then wrap the stem with white floral tape.

2. To prepare the ribbon loops that frame the bouquet, cut seven 6" lengths of white satin ribbon. On the wrong side measure 1½" from the left end of each piece and mark with a pencil. Fold the right end over to your pencil mark. Squeeze the two ends together in the center and secure by wrapping with white thread.

3. Pair up one (lavender) mini rose with one pearl stamen cluster, giving you three pairs. Incorporate the three wrapped almonds and the three pairs of roses and pearls into the purchased white mini-rose bouquet, alternating them between the flowers and leaves. Trim all stems to the same length, then wrap together with white floral tape from the top to the bottom of the stem.

4. Arrange the seven ribbon loops around the outside of the bouquet. Space them as evenly as possible (overlapping slightly) and wrap with white thread to secure them in place. You may want to do this in several steps. Wrap the stem again using white floral tape to incorporate the ends of the ribbon loops.

5. Cut a 28" length of ⅜" white satin ribbon to wrap the stem of the bouquet. Hold the ribbon in place at the top of the stem with your thumb and forefinger, leaving a 6" tail for the bow. Run the ribbon down the length of the stem and over the end, then begin to wrap, spiraling upward to where you started. Use a dab of hot glue to keep the ribbon from unwrapping. Thread the 6" ribbon tail through the hole in the printed message tag; tie the two ribbon ends together, then tie into a bow.

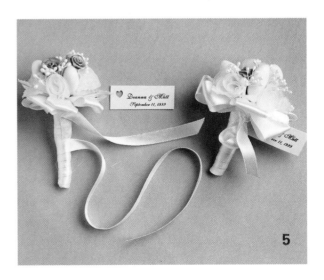

Party Menu

White wine

Assorted crudités

Aram sandwiches ★

Pepperoni pizza

Melon wedges

Floral cupcakes ★

Coffee, tea, herb tea

★*Recipe provided*

FLORAL CUPCAKES

(Makes 2 dozen cupcakes)

Prepare cupcakes using a purchased cake mix. Frost with Vanilla Buttercream Frosting (see below). Decorate with sugar flowers from a bakery supply or party store or make your own roses using sugar paste or chilled frosting squeezed from a pastry bag.

VANILLA BUTTERCREAM FROSTING

(Frosts 2 dozen cupcakes)

½ cup (1 stick) butter

4 cups powdered sugar, sifted

1 tablespoon vanilla

⅓ cup milk or cream

Stir the vanilla into the milk. Using a mixer, cream the butter until light and fluffy. Gradually add the sifted powdered sugar, then the milk, and beat until thick but still spreadable. Thin with a little more milk if needed.

ARAM SANDWICHES

(Makes 24 pieces, serves approx. 8)

1 package Lavosh bread, available at Middle Eastern markets, health food stores, and some grocery stores

For cream cheese filling

16 ounces cream cheese, softened

1 bunch scallions, chopped

2 tablespoons cream or milk

2 tablespoons dill, chopped

For sandwich fillings

8 ounces smoked salmon, thinly sliced

1 cup olives, chopped

1 head red lettuce, chopped

2 tomatoes, thinly sliced

½ recipe diced lemon chicken (page 80) or 8 ounces sliced pastrami

Stir the cream cheese filling ingredients together with a fork. Place each piece of Lavosh between two clean, damp tea towels for about half an hour to soften. When soft, carefully spread the cream cheese mixture atop each piece. Top with sandwich fillings as desired. Roll up each sandwich lengthwise, wrap in plastic wrap, and chill for 3 hours or overnight. Using a very sharp knife, cut each roll crosswise (diagonally) into eight pieces before serving.

Garden Party

ONCE UPON A TIME, NO PROPER YOUNG LADY WOULD dream of being led down the garden path for anything short of marriage. How perfectly wonderful! We have a garden path, and the garden itself, decked out to celebrate just that intent. From the pansy cutouts for the invitations to potted violas for the favors themselves, this chapter puts you on the right path to create a garden party of earthly delights. Of course, if you are the kind of person who loves nothing better than *pottering* around in a garden, you'll also enjoy potting springtime bulbs in terra cotta pots dressed up with flowers and ribbon.

Fortunately, a thriving spring or summer garden is its own glory, so let Nature have her pretty head with the decorations. Who better than Mother Nature to dress up the wedding season? Since you need not waste time improving the location, concentrate on setting the prettiest tables in the most beautiful spots, to take full advantage of the view.

Dress the tables with even more of nature's bounty, to admire and to eat. What is more delicious than garden-fresh vegetables, cooked lightly, then served in their own kingdom? A beautiful platter is a natural throne for delicate asparagus. Artichoke hearts, garnished with a rainbow of vegetables, bask on a thick slice of golden polenta. Even the poached salmon blooms with lovely lemon slices. Hearts already rejoicing will be fortified by this feast of beauty and health. ⸜

GARDEN PARTY INVITATION

SUPPLIES FOR EACH CARD:

(First, refer to Tips for Invitations on page 92.)

(Vellum) purchased envelope

(White) card stock

(White rice) paper

(Lavender rice) paper

(Green rice) paper

Color copies of flower illustrations

⅞"-wide (green) sheer ribbon

(Mauve metallic) thread

Decorative-edge (deckle) craft scissors

INSTRUCTIONS

1. Cut a piece of white card stock ¼" narrower than the width of the envelope and double the height of the envelope minus ¼". Fold in half.

2. Using (deckle edge) scissors cut out the next three layers: First, cut a piece of (white rice) paper to fit within the folded front of card; second, a square of (lavender rice) paper on point to fit within the (white rice) layer. Last cut out the large pansy illustration leaving a ⅛" border beyond the image. With the fold of the card at the top, center, layer and glue pieces in place as shown.

3. Tie metallic thread tightly around the center of a piece of (green) sheer ribbon. Hot-glue ribbon center to pansy motif where the two stems meet. Twist each ribbon end and glue midway along each length, positioning as shown. Trim ribbon ends in a decorative "V."

4. For the envelope, cut out a small pansy illustration. Using (deckle edge) scissors, cut a small square of (green rice) paper large enough to surround the pansy. Glue pansy to rice paper, then glue unit to envelope flap.

THE MENU

Strawberry lemonade
Poached salmon★
Fresh asparagus with vinaigrette
Polenta pizza★
Roasted red peppers and eggplant
Carrot cake★

★*Recipe provided*

POLENTA PIZZAS

(Makes 8-12 pizzas)

For the polenta

2 cups polenta

10 cups cold water or chicken broth

1 teaspoon salt (reduce or omit if using canned chicken broth)

¼ cup (½ stick) butter

2 cups grated Parmesan or Asiago cheese

For the topping

1 package frozen artichoke hearts

2 cloves garlic

2 tablespoons olive oil

8 ounces mozzarella cheese, grated

4 tomatoes, chopped

1½ cups pitted Kalamata olives

2 tablespoons fresh parsley, chopped

2 tablespoons fresh oregano, chopped

Olive oil for topping

Prepare the polenta crust. Butter a 12" x 17" jelly roll pan. In a large saucepan, combine the polenta and water or chicken broth. Slowly bring to a boil, stirring every minute or so. Reduce heat and simmer for 40 minutes, stirring every few minutes at first, more frequently as the polenta thickens. After 40 minutes, stir in the butter and cheese. Pour into the greased pan and let cool.

To assemble the pizzas

Sauté the artichokes and garlic together in the olive oil; add salt and pepper to taste. Have the other ingredients in separate bowls. Preheat the broiler. Using a 4" round cookie cutter, cut out pizza crusts from the polenta. Place on a greased cookie sheet and top each one with the artichoke mixture, tomatoes, olives, then cheese. Broil for about 4-6 minutes, until the cheese softens. Remove from the broiler and sprinkle with chopped herbs. Using a spatula, carefully transfer to a decorative plate and serve.

POACHED SALMON

(Serves 8)

3-pound salmon filet at room temperature

Salt and pepper to taste

3 medium lemons

Several sprigs of parsley, to garnish

Fill a large, shallow pan with several inches of water (enough to cover salmon). Bring to a boil, then carefully lower the salmon filet into the pan. Bring the water just to a simmer, not a hard rolling boil. Turn off the heat, cover the pan, and begin timing. For a rare salmon, leave 8 minutes; for completely cooked salmon, leave 10-11 minutes. Using a large spatula, carefully remove the filet and drain on paper towels. Cool, then place on a serving plate and refrigerate. Remove from the refrigerator about one hour before serving. Slice lemons paper-thin. Salt and pepper the salmon, then decorate with the lemon slices and parsley. Serve with your favorite vinaigrette.

CARROT CAKE

(Serves 12-14)

2 cups flour

2 teaspoons baking soda

2 teaspoons baking powder

2 teaspoons cinnamon

½ teaspoon salt

1¼ cups vegetable oil

2 cups granulated sugar

4 eggs, beaten

3 cups carrots, finely grated

½ cup each chopped walnuts, shredded coconut, raisins

Preheat oven to 325 degrees. Combine dry ingredients except sugar in mixing bowl. Wet ingredients should be at room temperature.

Stir vegetable oil, sugar, and eggs together, then add to dry ingredients, mixing thoroughly. Stir in carrots, walnuts, coconut, and raisins. Pour into two 9"-round greased cake pans. Bake for 30-40 minutes. Cool, then layer using frosting for filling. Top with cream cheese frosting.

To assemble the cake

Use a third of the frosting (recipe below) to fill the cake. Cover with the second layer. Frost the top and sides, saving about a quarter of the remaining frosting for decorating. Using a pastry bag fitted with a decorative tip, pipe a decorative ribbon around the edge of the cake. Gently press edible pansies and violas into the top and base of the cake.

CREAM CHEESE FROSTING

1½ cups (3 sticks) butter, softened

16 ounces cream cheese, softened

1 tablespoon lemon juice

Grated rind of 2 lemons

2¾ cups powdered sugar, sifted

Approx. 36 edible pansies and/or violas

Using an electric mixer at medium speed, blend the butter, cream cheese, lemon juice, and rind together until light and fluffy, about three minutes. Decrease speed to low and add the powdered sugar. If the frosting is too thick, thin with a few drops of lemon juice.

4. Pass along these growing instructions to your guests:

To prepare your paperwhite for blooming, remove the ribbon and place the saucer below the pot. Fill the bottom of the pot with ¼" of potting soil. Place the bulb on top then sprinkle more soil around it. Tap gently to settle the soil. Up to half of the bulb can be exposed. Put in a cool, sunny place indoors, or outdoors in zones 9-10. Water regularly, keeping moist but not soggy. The bulb will bloom in about a month.

Colorful violas are a garden favorite, perfect for sprucing up any party table. Landscape varieties are available in flats almost year-round and can be transplanted easily into small apothecary jars for guests to take home and enjoy after the party.

FLOWER BULB FAVORS

SUPPLIES FOR EACH FAVOR:

One paperwhite Narcissus bulb

One 3"-4" terra cotta pot with matching saucer

38" of ⅝"-wide satin ribbon

One fresh or silk paperwhite flower

1. Purchase paperwhite Narcissus bulbs at your favorite nursery. These wonderfully fragrant bulbs are available from September to January. The varieties Ziva and Galilee are the most reliable.

2. Place bulb in the terra cotta pot and cover with the saucer turned upside-down. As though you are wrapping a package, use the ribbon to tie the pot and saucer together, finishing with a bow on top. Slip a fresh or silk flower under the bow. Store in a cool, dry place until the party.

Mediterranean Party

YOU WORKED TIRELESSLY ORGANIZING THE WEDDING of your dreams down to the pin on the boutonniere and booking the perfect honeymoon. Now all you have to do is wait and wait. Caught you looking at the calendar again! For having outdone yourself in the efficiency category, you deserve a reward.

Wouldn't a week-long cruise on the Mediterranean be great right about now? Well, of course you don't have time for a real cruise; besides, you would have to pack. But there is nothing to prevent your friends from bringing the delights of the Mediterranean to you. The party starts with classic invitations in green and gold, beautifully decorated with the olive-bough art included in this section.

The décor, sturdy boxes covered with colorful peasant textiles or simply bright tablecloths and napkins, creates an unusual stage for displaying an array of delicacies one might easily find while traveling the sunny regions of Spain, Italy, and Portugal. Fresh and wonderfully different recipes will carry you off to rustic inns and romantic villas.

While enjoying the company of good friends, dig into an amazing sampler of olives and peppers, tear off chunks of crusty bread, dip into savory olive oils, and the troubles of the world will disappear—so will the wild mushroom polenta, an intriguing tapanade, and a light but filling pasta. Even the favors for your guests, bottles of vinegar fragrant with herbs, will set everyone dreaming of sunny hillsides and faraway places.

You don't even need to pack. Could anything be more perfect?

MEDITERRANEAN INVITATIONS

SUPPLIES FOR EACH CARD:

(First, refer to Tips for Invitations on page 92.)

CARD 1

(Metallic gold) purchased envelope

(Speckled ecru) card stock

(Patterned vellum) decorative paper

Copy of large olive medallion and olive illustration

18kt.-gold leafing pen

Decorative-edge (deckle) craft scissors

CARD 2

(Silver striped, flecked cream) purchased envelope

(Dull olive green) card stock

(Pressed leaf) decorative rice paper

(Metallic gold) paper

Copy of small olive medallion illustration

18kt.-gold leafing pen

INSTRUCTIONS

1. Cut a piece of either (ecru or olive) card stock ¼" narrower than the width of the envelope and double the height of the envelope minus ¼". Fold (ecru) paper in half. Draw a gold line along one short edge of the (olive) paper using the gold-leafing pen, then fold (olive) paper in half.

2. Using decorative-edged scissors, cut a piece of (vellum) paper to fit on the folded front of (ecru) card. Draw a gold line around edges with gold-leafing pen. Cut a piece of (rice) paper to fit within folded (olive) card. Center and glue each (vellum or rice) paper to the front of the respective card (see photo).

3. Cut out small medallion illustration allowing a ⅟₁₆" border beyond edge of motif. Glue illustration to (metallic gold) paper, then cut ⅛" beyond previous border. Cut out large medallion illustration along outline. Glue each illustration to its respective card, centered and spaced as shown in photos. Using the gold-leafing pen, draw a line around the large medallion illustration about ⅛" from the edge of the motif.

4. Cut out olive illustration leaving a ⅟₁₆" border beyond the edge of the motif. Glue motif to the (metallic gold) envelope flap.

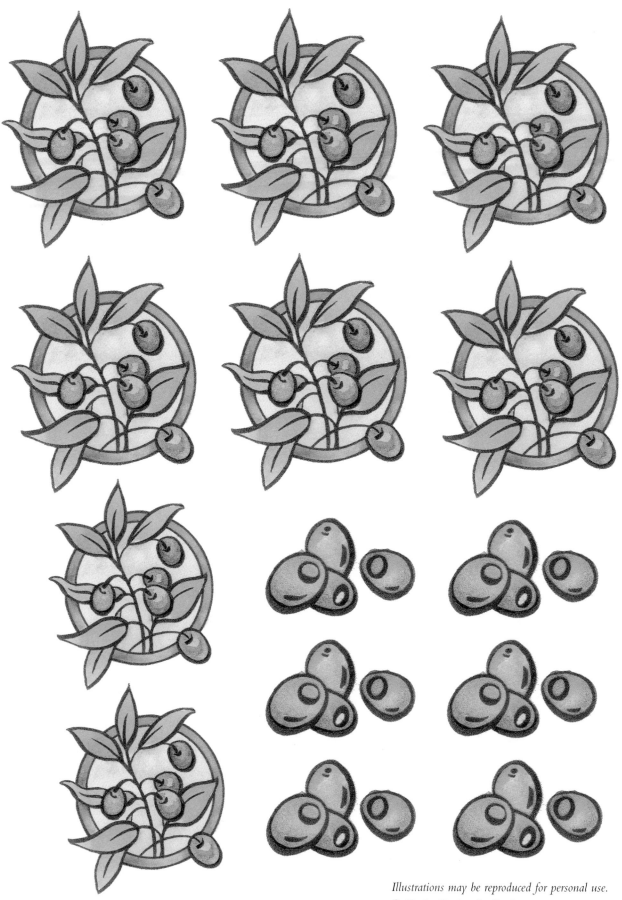

PARTY MENU

Chilled sangria with orange slices

Assorted cheeses and breads

Olives and pickled peppers

Mixed fruit salad

Green olive tapanade with pita toasts★

Pasta salad with grilled chicken★

Polenta with wild mushrooms★

Tiramisu

Espresso

★Recipe provided

POLENTA WITH WILD MUSHROOMS

(Serves 8)

For the polenta

Make the recipe for the polenta on page 64, except do not pour into the pan. Keep warm.

For the wild mushroom filling

    2 tablespoons butter

    2 tablespoons olive oil

    1 small yellow onion, or 3 large shallots, chopped

    2 cloves garlic, chopped

    1 pound mixed wild mushrooms, or a combination of wild and button mushrooms

    2 tablespoons fresh oregano or marjoram, chopped

    ½ cup Italian parsley, chopped

    Salt and pepper to taste

    ½ cup Parmesan cheese, grated, to garnish

In a frying pan, melt together butter and olive oil; add the onion or shallots. Sauté until soft, about 5 minutes. Add garlic and cook 30 seconds more. Add mushrooms and sauté until they lose their water. Salt and pepper to taste. Remove from heat, add herbs, and set aside.

To assemble

Butter an 8"-square baking pan. Pour a third of the warm polenta into the bottom. Top with half of the mushroom mixture. Add another third of the polenta mixture; top with remaining mushroom mixture. Add the final third of the polenta mixture on top and smooth with a spatula. Set aside for three hours or until firm, or refrigerate overnight.

To serve, bring to room temperature. Run a knife around the edges of the pan and turn out onto a board. Cut into quarters, then cut each piece in half, diagonally.

GREEN OLIVE TAPANADE
WITH PITA TOASTS

(Makes 4 cups)

5 cups green olives, pitted, rinsed and drained

¼ cup capers

⅓ cup red peppers, roasted, finely chopped

2 tablespoons garlic, finely chopped

2 tablespoons anchovies, finely chopped

⅔ cup ounces red onions, diced small

½ bunch Italian parsley washed, stemmed, and
   chopped

⅔ cup extra-virgin olive oil

Additional roasted red peppers for garnish

Add olives and capers to food processor; pulse to combine but not puree. Remove from food processor and combine with remaining ingredients. Make up to one week in advance. Garnish with red peppers on the day of serving. Serve with pita toasts.

PITA TOASTS

(Makes 48 wedges)

12-ounce package pita bread (6 pitas)

½ cup olive oil

Preheat the oven to 300 degrees. Brush each pita on both sides with olive oil. Cut into 8 pieces and place on a cookie sheet. Bake until crispy, about 45 minutes. Cool and store in an airtight container. Serve with tapanade.

PASTA SALAD

(Serves 8)

1 pound dried pasta—penne, twists, or bow ties

2 tablespoons olive oil

1 bunch basil or arugula

3 large or 6 medium tomatoes, chopped

½ recipe grilled lemon chicken (see page 80), cubed

1 cup Kalamata or other oil-cured olives, pitted and chopped

¼ cup pine nuts, toasted

Lemon garlic vinaigrette

Cook the pasta according to package directions. Toss with the olive oil and set aside to cool. Wash the basil or arugula. Tear the larger leaves in half, leaving the smaller ones whole. Toss with the cooled pasta, tomatoes, chicken, olives, and pine nuts. Pour about three quarters of the vinaigrette over the pasta salad and toss again. If the salad seems too dry, add remaining vinaigrette. Refrigerate, but bring to room temperature before serving.

LEMON VINAIGRETTE

1 cup extra-virgin olive oil

4 cloves garlic, chopped

¼ cup fresh lemon juice

¼ cup unseasoned rice vinegar

Salt and pepper to taste

Warm the olive oil in a saucepan and cook the garlic for about 30 seconds (avoid browning). Blend all the ingredients at high speed for about one minute.

FLAVORED VINEGAR FAVORS

Dress up your festivities with attractive bottles filled with fragrant herbed vinegar for your guests to take home. Small decorative bottles with locking tops can be purchased at import or kitchen stores, and a variety of fresh herbs are as close as your grocery or produce store.

Herbs such as thyme, tarragon, rosemary, bay, fennel, lemon balm, marjoram and savory (alone or in combination) are favorites for vinegars. Dried red peppers make an attractive presentation as well.

Loosely fill clean glass canning jars with the herbs, first bruising them slightly for more flavor. In a saucepan, warm enough white wine vinegar to fill the jars. Fill, then seal the jars tightly and set in a sunny window. Shake daily for two weeks, then strain the herbed vinegar through cheesecloth. Wash the small bottles thoroughly and fill with the vinegar. As a finishing touch, add a few fresh sprigs of herbs and a decorative tag with the names of the engaged couple.

Made For Each Other

QUICK! WHAT GOES WITH PEANUT BUTTER? JELLY, of course. Everybody knows that. Some combinations are so good, they are proverbial. This party is the perfect way to celebrate people who are made for each other.

As the wedding nears, people's minds tend to twosomes, so the party almost organizes itself. Favors are pairs of cheerful red felt hearts, bound together with red satin ribbons, adorning bottles of wine. Invitations are natural (of course!) colored paper, decorated with both applied and cutwork hearts.

The gifts are simply things that come to mind in pairs: candles or candlesticks, salt and pepper shakers, cups and saucers, bookends, pillowcases, his and her towels, matching pajamas or slippers, or anything else that leaps to your mind and brings a friend with it. There are even a few trios that are not out of place, such as silverware or china settings, mixing bowls, or even cans of tennis balls. After all, tennis is played in doubles!

The menu is a selection of foods that are happily paired. The main course consists of cleverly boxed suppers of finger foods for two, so that the cheerful couples can share the fun of the evening down to the last morsel. Even dessert comes in couples. Poached pears are a witty comment on the theme of the evening (see if anyone catches the little joke!).

Of course there must be music, and duets are the perfect choice. You can choose famous musical couples or happy couplings of instruments to set the mood. A quick browse through the local music store should provide delectable treats to suit every pair of ears. After an evening of delighting in happy couples, don't be surprised if the guests pronounce the evening "too, two perfect!"

MADE FOR EACH OTHER INVITATION

SUPPLIES FOR EACH CARD:

(First, refer to Tips for Invitations on page 92.)

(Flecked-sand) purchased envelope

(Flecked-sand) paper to match envelope

(Speckled-cream) paper for card

(Flecked decorative rice) paper

Raffia

Color copy of heart illustrations

Double-stick foam mounting tape

Decorative-edge (deckle) craft scissors

Decorative (⅝" heart) craft punch

INSTRUCTIONS

1. Cut a piece of (speckled-cream) paper ¼" narrower than the width of the envelope and double the height of the envelope minus ¼". Cut one short side using (deckle-edge) scissors. Fold in half.

2. Cut a piece of (flecked-sand) paper to fit on front of folded card. Along one short edge punch a row of three decorative (heart) shapes as shown. Center on front of folded card (deckle edge side), then glue in place.

3. Cut a piece of (rice) paper using (deckle-edge) scissors. The piece should fit within (flecked-sand) layer and above the decorative punched hearts as shown. Center and glue in place.

4. Cut out two large heart illustrations and a folded length of raffia. Arrange on (rice) paper. Hot-glue folded top and ends of raffia in place (see photo). Glue one heart over a raffia end. For a 3-D look use small pieces of double-stick foam tape to attach the second heart. Position it on the other raffia end, overlapping the first heart. Tie a raffia bow and hot-glue in place as shown.

5. Cut out one small pair of hearts and glue to a corner of the envelope flap.

PARTY MENU

Red wine

Crudités with herbed yogurt or Kalamata olive hummus

Parmesan breadsticks

Grilled lemon chicken with

Roquefort dipping sauce★

Fennel, blood orange, and arugula salad

Vanilla cheesecake★

Pecan pie★

Poached vanilla pears★

Individual iced coffees

★Recipe provided

GRILLED LEMON CHICKEN

(Serves 8)

8 boneless, skinless chicken breasts

1 cup lemon juice

¼ cup olive oil

1 teaspoon fresh thyme, chopped

Put the chicken breasts into a shallow bowl. Pour over the lemon juice and olive oil. Sprinkle the thyme over all. Cover and marinate in the regrigerator for several hours or overnight. When ready to grill, bring chicken to room temperature. Heat a ridged grill pan until very hot. Pat the chicken dry with paper towels and grill on high heat until done, about 5-7 minutes on each side. (Or grill the chicken breasts on an outdoor grill.) Cool the chicken and cut lengthwise into strips. Serve with Roquefort dipping sauce.

ROQUEFORT DIPPING SAUCE

4 ounces cream cheese, softened

1 tablespoon lemon juice

4 ounces Roquefort cheese

½ cup mayonnaise

½ cup cream

Blend all ingredients at high speed for one minute, or until combined. Serve with lemon chicken.

Everyone loves a great cheesecake (opposite), and this one, topped with fresh raspberries, is perfection (recipe on page 82).

VANILLA CHEESECAKE

(Serves 8)

Prepare the cheesecake the day before the party so that the flavors can develop overnight.

For the crust

1½ cups graham cracker crumbs

½ cup (1 stick) butter, melted

For the cheesecake

24 ounces cream cheese, softened

1½ cups sugar

4 eggs at room temperature

1 tablespoon vanilla

For the topping

2 cups sour cream

½ cup sugar

2 teaspoons vanilla

½ pint fresh raspberries

12-ounce package unsweetened frozen
  raspberries (optional)

Preheat the oven to 350 degrees. Mix the graham cracker crumbs and butter together and pat into the bottom of a 9" springform pan. On low speed of mixer, combine the cream cheese and sugar until blended. Add the eggs one at a time, then the vanilla. Pour the filling into the crust and bake for 35-40 minutes, or until just set. Remove from oven; cool at least 15 minutes.

For the topping, mix sour cream, sugar and vanilla until combined. Pour atop of slightly cooled cheesecake in an even layer. Place in 450-degree oven for 10 minutes. Cool half an hour; remove side of springform pan and refrigerate.

Before serving

Decorate the cake with the fresh raspberries and/or serve with a raspberry sauce. To make sauce, heat one package frozen raspberries in a small saucepan, adding up to 2 tablespoons of sugar. Let cool. Puree in a blender until smooth, strain then chill. To serve, spread a tablespoon of sauce on each plate or drizzle a zigzag pattern from a spoon. Top with a slice of cheesecake.

PECAN PIE

(Serves 8)

1 cup dark brown sugar

1 cup light corn syrup

⅓ cup melted butter

½ teaspoon salt

1 teaspoon vanilla

3 eggs, slightly beaten

1 deep-dish, 9" pre-made frozen pie shell or
  make your own pie shell using the quiche crust
  recipe on page 22

1 heaping cup pecan halves

Preheat oven to 350 degrees. In a large mixing bowl, combine the brown sugar, corn syrup, melted butter, salt, and vanilla; stir well. Add the eggs and beat the mixture using an electric mixer for 2-3 minutes. Pour the mixture into a 9" unbaked deep-dish pie shell. Sprinkle the pecans evenly over the top. Bake at 350 degrees for 45 minutes, or until the pie is firm. Let the pie cool before cutting and serving.

POACHED VANILLA PEARS

(Serves 8)

8 medium pears, slightly under-ripe

4 cups sugar

4 cups water

3 whole vanilla beans, split lengthwise

8 vanilla beans for garnish (optional)

Peel pears, leaving stems intact. Prepare a syrup by mixing sugar and water. Place pears upright in a deep saucepan and pour the syrup over them, covering completely. If you need more syrup to cover the pears, add equal parts water and sugar. Add the split vanilla beans. Slowly bring to a simmer. Continue to simmer until pears are barely cooked through, and still slightly firm (about 20 minutes). Cool in the syrup. When cool, carefully remove to a serving plate. Return the syrup to the stove and simmer until reduced by half. Cool, then pour a few tablespoons over the cooled pears. Refrigerate or set aside until ready to serve. If refrigerated, bring to room temperature before serving. Garnish with vanilla beans, if desired.

PAIR OF HEARTS TIE-ONS

SUPPLIES FOR EACH PAIR

Four squares of 3½" x 3½" red felt

⅔ yard of ⅛"-wide red satin ribbon

Lightweight paper

Red embroidery floss and needle

Straight pins

Polyester fiberfill

Hot glue

INSTRUCTIONS

1. Cut a 8½" length of ribbon.

2. Trace the pattern for the heart onto folded paper, cut out, then unfold.

3. Pin paper pattern to two felt squares. Cut around pattern. Repeat with remaining two felt squares.

4. Using a blanket stitch (see below) and two strands of red floss, stitch two of the felt hearts together, starting at the bottom point. Work around to the center notch, then insert one end of the red satin ribbon between the pieces of felt. Be sure to catch the ribbon with one of your stitches. Continue to stitch to within 1" of your starting point.

5. Stuff the hearts lightly with polyester fiberfill, then complete stitching.

6. For the other heart, repeat steps 4 and 5, inserting the opposite end of the ribbon between the pieces of felt. Keep the ribbon flat between the two hearts (no twists).

7. Cut the remaining piece of ribbon into two equal pieces, then tie each piece into a bow. Using hot glue, attach a bow to each heart as shown in the photo.

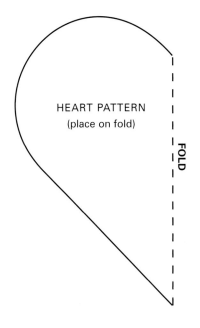

HEART PATTERN
(place on fold)

FOLD

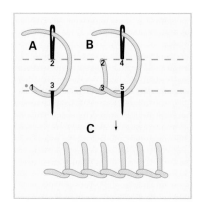

BLANKET STITCH

Rehearsal Dinner

IT IS THE NIGHT BEFORE THE WEDDING. PLANS ARE complete. The trip to the altar has reached the final stage, and slows to a stately pace before the walk down the aisle. One duty remains, and that is giving the Rehearsal Dinner.

Traditionally, the groom's parents provide the rehearsal dinner for all the wedding attendants, their spouses, and the immediate families of the bride and groom. It is thoughtful to include the officiating clergy and their spouses and the wedding musicians if they participate in the rehearsal. Sometimes the friends of an older betrothed couple give this dinner as one of the prenuptial parties, or as a wedding gift.

In recent years the definition of "immediate family" has been extended to include the escorts of wedding attendants as well as family members and guests from out of town. This is a matter of personal taste and practicality, as well as budget.

Too often the groom's family members are perceived as guests on the fringes of the bride's glory. Nothing is further from the truth. This is a tribal moment. The groom is receiving the treasured child of the bride's family. His family are there to show the bride's parents the esteem in which their daughter is held. As much as the bride's parents are anxious to carry off the wedding in fine form, the groom's parents want to do things properly at the rehearsal dinner.

The groom's family may be at a disadvantage if they come from a different town from the bride's family and must provide hospitality away from home. Designating a bridesmaid or two to help the groom's mother with dinner arrangements or navigating an unfamiliar town would be an act of kindness, and the bride's parents will be relieved of yet another responsibility during a busy time.

Because the rehearsal dinner is the best opportunity for the groom's family to offer hospitality to the family and friends of the bride, it is a courtesy to send invitations. They can be formal or tastefully informal. Aside from providing a written document to avoid mix-ups of the time and location, invitations also tell the bridal attendants and ushers that they are honored guests at the joining of two families.

SETTING THE TIME

Since this dinner follows the wedding rehearsal, plan the rehearsal for afternoon or early evening. The amount of time planned for the rehearsal may depend on the schedule of the officiant or wedding site. If possible, schedule a few hours for the rehearsal and allow extra time to get to the dinner location when fixing the hour for the meal to begin.

Dinner should occur before the wedding participants drop from hunger, and so they have a chance of getting a reasonable night's sleep. It is a good idea to designate one of the groomsmen or bridesmaids as the official timekeeper, so that the wedding party can keep the rehearsal and the party somewhat on schedule.

Consider having photos and videotapes taken of the rehearsal frolics, to be added to the collection from the wedding day itself. In fact, you may get the best performance from the flower girl and ring bearer during the rehearsal. It would be a shame to lose the fun for want of a camera. If the parents are at the rehearsal, having them snap some photos gives them something fun to do.

CHOOSING A LOCATION

Where to hold the rehearsal dinner depends on a number of variables: how many people will be attending, where the wedding is to be held, and what restaurants are in the vicinity. Hiring a private dining room and having the dinner catered is a great idea. After the wedding preparations, families of the bride and groom will enjoy some quiet time together on the eve of the festivities. Like the engagement party, everyone can become better acquainted. Toasts will be offered, speeches made, and guests will be touched with emotion.

The location chosen for a rehearsal dinner also determines the menu. If you are in a city with lots of good restaurants, take your choice. Any restaurant that can accommodate your group and serve everyone good food in a reasonable amount of time will do. A pre-arranged menu may speed up the service, as well as fix the costs in advance. For a larger group of diners many chefs will prepare dishes not normally available.

For a picnic on the prairie, picnic fare is logical. But if a picnic is the logical choice it can still be fabulous and memorable, especially if catered by a specialist in gourmet meals at remote sites. You can even have a delightful picnic in the city. A hotel rooftop is no less *al fresco*, just because it is twenty floors up. The change of view may be just what everyone needs to keep things in perspective.

HONORING YOUR PARENTS

Other things also change your perspectives. No matter how old you are, marriage alters the relationship with your parents. It is a joyful change, and at the same time, a poignant one: a change which deserves to be formally acknowledged. You may want to commemorate this with some small ceremony of thanks to your parents and a handmade token of love.

A touching one might be the thoughtful preparation of a book of memories for each set of parents. These are the son's or daughter's own memories, illustrated with photos, clippings, sketches, or drawings in the margins, even stick figures. The memories can be anything that was important or special from your childhood: your relationship with your parents, funny pranks that they never found out about, or how they helped you through events that they may not even remember. Your mother may have led you to become a mathematician just by teaching you how to work with fractions as she made dinner. Your father may have explained the meaning of what became your favorite poem. Anything that you remember fondly is worth including.

Such memories can evoke riotous laughter or tears of understanding and they are a fitting tribute to parents on the eve of a momentous change. By building a bridge to yesterday you can reassure them that some things will never change.

HANDCRAFTING A MEMENTO

In this chapter we include directions for making silk scarves and pocket squares as mementos of the evening. Though gifts are customarily given to the wedding attendants, these scarves and pocket squares are so nice that everyone would be delighted to receive one. With the tears of the evening and the following day, you cannot make too many pocket squares, for the ladies as well as the gentlemen. And they are so inexpensive and simple to do that you will have fun making them long after you have more than enough. Generosity is the nature of love; give in to it wholeheartedly.

You have worked hard to plan a wedding perfect in every detail, to be remembered forever. An equally well-planned rehearsal dinner will relax and refresh everyone, setting the stage to celebrate love's vows the next day. Here's to "Forever!"

LOVE AND FRIENDSHIP SILK GIFTS

Hand-painted Scarves and Gentlemen's Squares

DESIGNED BY DEBORAH PADRICK

SUPPLIES

9" x 54" 8mm habotai silk pre-hemmed white scarves
(refer to page 93 for source)

11" x 11" silk squares cut from any silk fabric; pre-
hemmed or add rolled hem using silk thread

Dye colors by *Jacquard Silk Colors* (60 ml size)

Blue design: yellow, turquoise, royal, purple, viridian

Peach design: poppy, magenta, purple

(for light colors dilute with water, about 1 part dye to
3 parts water)

Dye set by *Jacquard* (250 ml) (if using another dye
brand, note setting instructions)

Gutta resist by *Jacquard*

Blue design: Silver (use medium nib)

Peach design: Gold (use small nib)

(clear gutta may also be used for either design)

Ice-cube-tray palette and eye dropper

(For stretching silk) set of wooden stretcher bars (to
match size of silk square) and pushpins or masking
tape and straight pins (for scarf)

Soft bristled brushes (bamboo brushes work well)

Squeeze bottles with small and medium nibs

INSTRUCTIONS

Applying the Design

1. Iron the silk using medium heat. Stretch and suspend
the silk square across wooden stretcher bars and
secure with push pins. For the scarf, put 3" tabs of masking tape on all four corners of the silk, straight-pin the
tape to the silk, then suspend the scarf between two
metal or plastic chairs using the tape to hold the silk to
the chairs at the corners.

2. Draw squiggly lines and hearts using a squeeze bottle with a small or medium metal nib and metallic gutta
resist. The resist separates color areas and develops the
design. (If you're new to this technique, plan your design

on a piece of paper first.) Personalize by writing any message you'd like. Draw with resist directly onto the silk. The resist nib should touch the silk fabric as you draw. It's important to apply even, flowing lines with no gaps. If the design goes off the edge of the scarf, put a dab of resist on the back of the hem. Check your completed design to make sure the gutta has penetrated the back of the fabric. Reapply gutta to close any gaps in the lines.

3. Allow the resist to dry thoroughly before painting with dye. Place a small amount of dye in an ice-cube-tray palette using an eye dropper; dilute dyes with water for pastel colors (test on white paper or a scrap of white silk). With experience, you may wish to mix colors to coordinate with your wedding colors. Using a different soft bristled brush for each color, apply the colored dyes evenly and quickly; work in strokes that overlap by about ¼" for even coverage. When painting silk yardage, play with blending and overlapping colors. The colors will flow into each other on the fabric like watercolors. To prevent unwanted water lines, finish each area before dyes are allowed to dry completely. Clean brushes in water.

Setting the Dyes

4. You must set the dyes to ensure permanence. This can be done as soon as the painted silk is completely dry or at a later time. Prepare two or more quarts of solution in a clean tub or container. Use one ounce of *Jacquard Dye Set Solution* per quart of cold water. (Dye set can be re-used.) Fill a second container with plain cold water. Quickly immerse the painted silk scarf in the dye set solution; slosh for a few minutes, then immerse in plain cold water.

5. To dry, drape the rinsed silk scarf over an old sheet stretched over metal or plastic chairs, or over a towel on your shower curtain rod. (Keep as free of wrinkles as possible.) While silk is still damp, cover an ironing board with a cotton sheet, then iron using medium heat.

6. The pieces are ready to wear and can be hand washed. Do not dry clean metallic or colored gutta resist; it will dissolve. You may wish to remove clear gutta resist by dry cleaning, but it's not necessary.

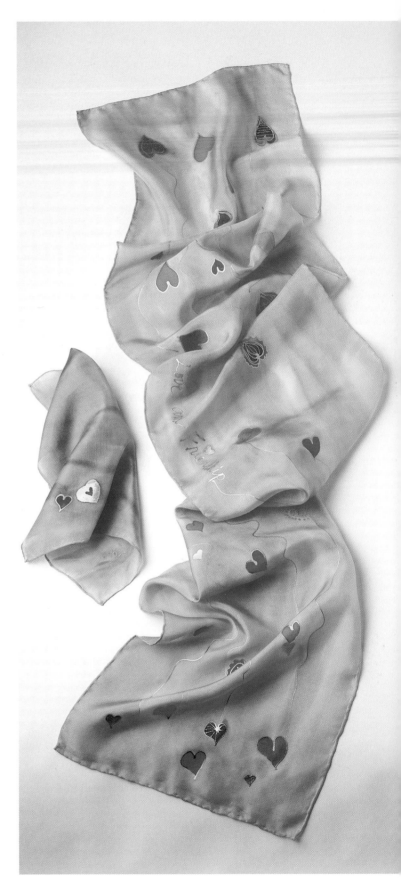

CREATE YOUR OWN INVITATIONS

GENERAL INSTRUCTIONS

To create your personalized invitations, start with purchased envelopes from your local stationery, art, craft, or memory bookstore. To this, add a purchased blank card or custom cut one to fit the envelope. The card paper should be ¼" (6mm) narrower and ¼" (6mm) shorter than double the height of the accompanying envelope (unless otherwise instructed.)

You may substitute the color of your paper, weight and type, as well as the decorative effects and embellishments as desired. We offer suggestions printed within parentheses in the card supply lists. Determine amounts of supplies required by multiplying the number of invitations by the card size and the estimated size and number of embellishments from the individual invitation supply list.

PAPER AND EMBELLISHMENTS

You can choose from an amazing variety of papers. Here are some tips to help you make your selections: Choose paper that carries out the theme and colors of your party. Select a heavy parchment, card or cover stock or even a watercolor paper for your card. Add interest to the purchased or custom card by layering lighter weight papers of various textures and transparencies. Textured papers do not take printing well. Choose a smooth paper stock to print your event details, then mount it on the textured stock.

Incorporate embellishments such as ribbon, lace, pressed flowers, feathers, buttons, and charms into your design. Add stickers or sealing wax to the envelope. Even your postage stamp can be an embellishment.

ILLUSTRATIONS

You are permitted to reproduce the invitation illustrations in this book for your personal use only. Print as many as you need using a color copier or a home computer, scanner and printer.

TOOLS AND CRAFT SUPPLIES

Here is a list of basic tools that are needed for most of the invitations. Special-effect tools are listed with their individual invitation supply lists.

- Cutting tool—paper cutter, rotary cutter, or craft knife (to cut several sheets of paper at one time)
- Ruler
- Straight edge to cut against
- Cutting mat
- Hot glue gun
- Glue stick
- White craft glue

PARTY PARTICULARS

Write event details directly inside card or add a separate sheet using handwritten or computer-generated information. A decorative way to attach an insertion is to punch aligned holes through the sheet and back of card with a long-reach punch. Thread ribbon through the holes, tying the layers together.

RESOURCES

SPECIALTY FOODS

OAKVILLE GROCERY

Barbara Henderson, Manager

Erin Vreeland, Chef

1352 Locust Street

Walnut Creek, CA 94596

Tel 925-274-7900

Fax 925-274-7909

Page 73

HAND-PAINTED SILK

SILKART

Deborah Padrick

P.O. Box 847

Forestville, CA 95436

Tel 707-823-8153

Email debsilk@sonic.net

www.deborahsilk.com

Pages: 90-91

FLOWERS

IMPRESSIONS FLORAL DESIGN GALLERIA

2 Theatre Square, #136

Orinda, CA 94563-3346

Tel 925-253-0250

Fax 925-253-9946

RECIPE CREDITS

PAGE 13: Tea Sandwiches – Joanne Lehrer, Sebastopol, CA

PAGE 14: Chocolate-dipped Strawberries, Chocolate Truffles – Joanne Lehrer, Sebastopol, CA

PAGE 15: Lemon Bars – Joanne Lehrer, Sebastopol, CA; Coconut Macaroons – Sandy Orton, Rodeo, CA

PAGE 22: Mimosas, Spinach Quiche – Joanne Lehrer, Sebastopol, CA

PAGE 24: Cream Scones – Joanne Lehrer, Sebastopol, CA; Quick Clotted Cream, Quick Devonshire Cream, Easy Old-fashioned Lemon Curd – Sandy Orton, Rodeo, CA

PAGE 40: Easy Chicken Divan – Basha Hanner, Oakland, CA

PAGE 41: Lemonade – Joanne Lehrer, Sebastopol, CA

PAGE 42-43: Lemon Meringue Tarts – Sandy Orton, Rodeo, CA

PAGE 50: Quick Blini – Joanne Lehrer, Sebastopol, CA

PAGE 52: Ultimate Chocolate Cake – Lorelie Barth, Canton, SD

PAGE 58: Aram Sandwiches – Joanne Lehrer, Sebastopol, CA

PAGE 59: Vanilla Buttercream Frosting – Joanne Lehrer, Sebastopol, CA

PAGE 64: Polenta Pizzas, Poached Salmon – Joanne Lehrer, Sebastopol, CA

PAGE 66: Carrot Cake – Shelley Carda, Piedmont, SD; Cream Cheese Frosting – Joanne Lehrer, Sebastopol, CA

PAGE 72: Polenta with Wild Mushrooms – Joanne Lehrer, Sebastopol, CA

PAGE 73: Green Olive Tapanade – Erin Vreeland, Chef, Oakville Grocery, Walnut Creek, CA; Pita Toasts – Joanne Lehrer, Sebastopol, CA

PAGE 74: Pasta Salad – Joanne Lehrer, Sebastopol, CA

PAGE 80: Grilled Lemon Chicken, Roquefort Dipping Sauce – Joanne Lehrer, Sebastopol, CA

PAGE 82: Vanilla Cheesecake – Jorja Hernandez, Glendale, UT; Pecan Pie – Bé Aspinwall, Cherry Creek, CO

PAGE 84: Poached Vanilla Pears – Joanne Lehrer, Sebastopol, CA

PHOTO CREDITS

DIANNE WOODS

1041 Folger St.

Berkeley, CA 94710

Tel 510-841-9220

FRONT AND BACK COVERS
PAGES: 4, 5 , 6, 10, 11, 13, 14, 15, 16, 18, 20, 22, 23, 25, 26, 27, 28, 29, 30, 33, 35, 36, 38, 40, 41, 43, 44, 46, 48, 51, 52, 53, 54, 56, 57, 58, 59, 60, 62, 65, 66, 67, 68, 70, 72, 73, 74, 75, 76, 78, 80, 81, 83, 84, 85, 87, 89, 90, 91

DON FRASER

1041 Folger St.

Berkeley, CA 94710

Tel 510-841-9220

PAGE 12: Jennifer Orzell and Jeff Murrish, private home, Piedmont, CA

PAGE 55: Michelle Manick and Ken Daxter, Sonoma Golf Club, Sonoma, CA

PAGE 86: Cookie Endicott and John Britton, Silicon Valley Capital Club, San Jose, CA

PAGE 88: Jody Wrath and Andrew Palmigiano, San Rafael, CA

INDEX

INDEX